TRAFFIC & WEATHER

FUTUREPOEM BOOKS
NEW YORK CITY
2008

TRAFFIC & WEATHER

MARCELLA DURAND

FIRST EDITION | FIRST PRINTING

This edition first published in paperback by Futurepoem books
www.futurepoem.com
Series Editor: Dan Machlin
Guest Editors: Laura Elrick, Rob Fitterman and Tonya Foster

Cover Design: Mickel Design (http://www.mickeldesign.com)

Cover images: Crowd photo: British Ministry of Information, 1942;
Sun photo: ESA./NASA/SOHO, 1999.

Typesetting & copyediting: *typeslowly* (cjmattison@gmail.com)

Cover font is Feijoa. Text set in Scala.
Printed in the United States of America on acid-free paper.
Signature Book Printing, www.sbpbooks.com

This project is supported in part by the New York State Council on the Arts, a state agency,
the New York Community Trust, and the Fund for Poetry. Futurepoem receives nonprofit
sponsorship for grants and donations through Fractured Atlas Productions, Inc., a 501(c)3
tax exempt organization. Contributions are fully tax-deductible and much needed!

NYSCA
New York State Council on the Arts

Distributed to the trade by Small Press Distribution, Berkeley, California
Toll-free number (U.S. only): 800.869.7553
Bay area/International: 510.524.1668
orders@spdbooks.org
www.spdbooks.org

ACKNOWLEDGMENTS:

Traffic & Weather was written from November 2005 to May 2006 as part of a residency at the Lower Manhattan Cultural Council. The residency was located at 120 Broadway where I worked alongside 12 visual artists; some of their working practices can be found within the poem. One excerpt was published as part of a collaborative postcard with Edwin Torres, my fellow writer-in-residence. Many thanks to Erin Donnelly and the LMCC.

My gratitude also to Marjorie Welish, Brenda Coultas, Elaina Ganim, Jo Ann Wasserman, and Bradford Morrow for their editorial input. Thanks also to the Futurepoem judges: Laura Elrick, Rob Fitterman, Tonya Foster, and Dan Machlin (also my publisher).

Parts of *Traffic & Weather* have appeared in *Big Bridge*, *The Canary*, *Conjunctions*, *The Denver Quarterly*, and *Sal Mimeo*. One section was published by Farfalla Press as a broadside with art by George Schneeman and another was published in *For the Time Being: The Bootstrap Book of Poetic Journals*, Bootstrap Productions, 2007.

To Richard O'Russa and Ismael Toussaint Durand O'Russa

a gentle curve takes over   when the spine unbends a bit and is kneaded
        and here you are, with light striking off concaves and convexes
in a gleaming moment before lamp is turned off   it's growing late and time to call
        look out the window and think there once was a guy in Russia
        or if we were going to argue in one more moment

        time to call   when this song is over or if I can make it to the corner
before the door opens and neighbors spill out   in five minutes or just a half-hour
when under a time constraint   a deadline   a CD spins for a second when lid
is opened   a CD is a compact disc in case you read this when they are
obsolete   many metals went into their making supposedly they disintegrate

in 10 years or another hour   here comes the part of the tune you like   I could
stop or pause walk by the wall   and maybe cornices will catch the rain
a skylight is an interesting construction   reminiscent of factories in Switzerland
That there are industrial buildings in Europe   jars the romantic image of small
Grecian huts or thatched roofs and not a collage and instead comes

from everything we remembered from yesterday or sat here looking up at the sky-
light wondering if it's going to rain and break this heat wave rain gutters cisterns
storm overflow city water filtration plant   blocks and blocks and blocks and blocks
would be in rows but are uneven   from hill they appear as box   after months
in the wilderness le corbusian forms having razed the meadow and put 31 stories in
or after the x in orange circle denotes spot where wrecking ball
is to be   positioned

a city explores itself in boxes   just as a person is centered by circles

how does one step outside of one's block   glimpses of many
within one   as a place shivers and becomes many others   we leave
      our block   and become as one among many others

placed after wilderness comes the white bridge   closed off at third avenue
      the neighborhood divides onto second avenue and then onto first   river
drive at night and is never dark   kayakers paddle softly about tugboats and giant
cruise ships several stories high as they pass apartment building windows of
concrete blocks   and two holes prop up your drainage pipe it will clog under the
      makeshift mud hill now scattered with jewelweed   and poison ivy
      one cancels the other   if one touches

you the other will take to your skin with small yellow florets   as romanesque broccoli
is the same structure of deep sea mollusk shell   spinning upward   if in
one more moment we are going to argue   turn out the light   it rests my eyes
thinking if I am going to read

      because of the tune you like   another CD is wrecked   it's all stalled
if you think I am influenced   look for a millisecond as though it were *wooded*
here nature writes its own photo   ink-jets to a page made of something much like
itself   would have looked like before it was chopped
      and here you are tree   stay still for your rendition

if you think for one minute I'm going to wait   for an argument   here, *take* the fork
and not the digging tools   this acre was marked off and plants observed. Here is
my conclusion: Each and every one of them is an invasive alien.
That, plus a few aluminum cans, crushed.   Many of them will fit into a sac when
informed *Carry In, Carry Out*

4

or that's what he snapped at me as I lifted the garbage from the canoe and walked over to the ranger station, hoping for a trash can. We drank 30 beers while waiting on the island for daybreak. We didn't sleep, we waited. And in the morning, a mist covered the waters and the birds. It's here, *in a bowl*, a semi-circle, or really a *full circle* with few outlets, the river is hidden behind a small peninsula and reveals itself as *the forested banks part suddenly* and with a current, we are in

it was like that in the dream, except I had been given tasks: I was to classify trees and write them down except I had no paper and whether I was to turn the trees into paper I was not sure except I had to count them first, and lost track and lost track

it was when strapped into a subway and going down the gullet   I didn't have something in my purse that I always had   and this meant I had to
        face something without it
        then the dream brightened and I came out into a yard

when I turned over and described the dream to you, you were thinking about the clock

distraction, you said, and time   I said, it's about the trip   it quickly gets dull describing your own consciousness, but I would like to know what the dream "means"   do *you* know what the dream "means"?

we came down along what could have been a peninsula, triangulated
between one lake and another.

It could have been a bowl or a saucer, and if you tipped one side a little,
water came in. We used to talk about it when passing under trees.

cats disappeared and one blue jay outside the window squawked
in the mornings

or late in the evening, a petrochemical plant exhaled odor over the low roofs

city lights went on into a disappearing horizon

if we walk along when it is just becoming dawn
we can see where the city ends and wilderness begins

lights stop at a line and then it is dark
a tiny car, recognizable only by headlights, goes and is swallowed up

it was here that it was wrecked   and I haven't been back since
people talk about going   but we're not sure they are letting them in
it was condemned and now part of it is missing   spraypainted orange
along the sidewalks, this is where the cable will go   be careful of your street

she walks and walks, seeing many wonderful things and some terrible too
a fight between men that she breaks up
a floor lifting up when someone moves
long lines of light still vivid in the early morning
a lighter gray against gray

there is always time and never time
to be somewhere on time
each five minutes has an impingement
a curve takes over

tones of light still long in the morning seeing many things and some terrible too
it was missing and now this is where the cable goes before the long blast and two
short blasts   oval steel parts are lifted into the dynamited cavern as foundations
shift like granite shifts

if I were putting in a deep foundation and had purchased air   she walks past
and hears a whistle behind her   it could be a warning or the ground moves
the street lifts in a kind of ripple   and continues to where direction changes

the grey skylight gives a sense of reality
I had thought of something last night that had to do with an arrangement of groups
it was very beautiful and now all forgotten
it was surface and now it is deep
submerged and without oxygen
the giant striped fish comes up to us and inhales deeply
it inhales salty water and iodine is poisonous to crabs

as a factory as we are muscles
to trawl for many miles it will never fight back
even as we pin it down and make it take it
with outrage in its eyes
it looks at us mutely

even if you couldn't wait, could you?   if I let you go will you tell it to
someone   every five minutes has an impingement

I feel like complaining. Let me complain.
I'll fill this page with long lines of complaint.
Make it hard for me and I'll make it impenetrable for you.
It's not pretty and it's not orderly.
No music and certainly no harmoniums.
That's the way it is in the ocean: silent, blue and deep
or so say the whales, after sonar destroys their
eardrums, giant thumping sources of information

The ground is topographical and when dismantled reveals relics of inhabitants
upon inhabitants: Brass fronting or granite shell over rubble core, sheer glass over
interior steel ribbing, 24/7 company logo lights up dark block or block thought
to be dark before 24/7 company logo. No public clocks. Simple lighting works as
well—Deskeys or SLECOs with no ornament on their base. Deskeypoles (Street
Light Equipment Company). Points of commonality. Deskey designed Radio City
Music Hall as well as SLECO street lighting; Roebling designed smaller bridge(s)
over Delaware. All are pedestrian. Walkable. A source for crossing land.
Granite and spring wires tensile. Possibility of unravel but tight and frozen. Flows
of suspension energy seeming still, even as support is channeled into piles and
down into bedrock (or sand).

If which part is equal to   some things must be considered   what does this
represent   what street furnishing is   utilitarian   slapped together   or mean
to present or represent power, reason, or authority   the plastic newspaper boxes
or signs stapled (posted) on various poles: each pole several postings posted to it

or what would a trailer be like, as a movable space?
Is the city movable? or just impacted and layered   an empty space on wheels
shoddy and uninsulated   heater in space   a place looked at with nostalgia:
it happened here

SLECOs trail off into distance: on other side of river lie malls, developments, new
roads, and a mysterious malfunction. It opens and closes with no warning at all.

It had an aspect of you just as an exact chord does or a change in light. Light is gray
when coming through a skylight and is otherwise slightly tinged blue or white (in
this area). In another part, it is yellow and blurs the edges of everything. A small
image. Conveys something. Too much weight to convey anything.

SLECOs trail off into distance. Indicate something of destination. The older part
of the city gives way to new construction. Marked with an X where wrecking ball
should go. A chance to stand up once in a while and look out the window. Is it too
simple to say on one side the past and the other the future?

> But that is the view outside my window
> On one side is a graveyard belonging to one of the city's first churches
> On the other is a sculpture dedicated to one of the city's worst disasters
> then the disaster site itself

> Even here it looks like exposed wires
> sticking out of sand. A supporting wall and a chain-link fence. Water
> stains wall and now it is raining—the ground is puddled and dark.
> It is not rebuilt and not likely to be so soon.

Groups of people look at it; cars on the highway slow down.
They have forgotten about their "destination."
The sights of their travels are more interesting to them.

It is not rebuilt and not likely. Unlikely to build in this spot. A man writes "sight"
and "site" over and over, thinking it might lead somewhere. You misunderstand
this. Sight is too close to site. A sight cannot be on top of a site. One site cannot be
in the same sight as another site. Too many times is it written and for too long.

they trail into the distance   SLECOs are sometimes single, sometimes double
illuminating two streets at once or covering twice   as much distance.
Funding is disputed has no lighting and   a garden for which
ownership is debated will be razed or not razed   the garden was for a non-profit
housing project you thought it was visually purposeful   it doubled back on itself
being an accident or a coincidence   strange to avoid and almost
impossible as is a spiral staircase in every house   or city and so why not another?
We rush to pour the foundation before   zoning laws change why stop for
quality control? But it grows ragged.   You can't deny it grows ragged. At
times you are   a wall   or there is no way through you
you take it as denotative   you should leave a path, an "x" as to where to unbuild you

the mysterious site: a blasting zone and enormous coils of steel placed, drapes of
reinforced vinyl, plywood, blockaded, under city auspices, metal signs with number
of whistles   before the long blast and two short blasts   oval steel parts
into the cavern   as foundation shifts like granite drapes and some barbed wire
next to the very old building, reinforced   before it slides into the giant hole
if the quarry were turned to other uses, or just left alone   to slowly fill with water

Electricity makes us work.   The floor is not pretty yet. When will the elevator be
        questionable again? If you trail off.   Maybe we feel too significant.
        Muted and electronic distortion-double phase, battery low.
        Like I was by myself, music stops but tune continues. A series of small jokes.

        Where to unbuild you. Shadows of thumbtacks on walls. Bare line where
        paint missed. Electricity makes us work. Deli hands me too many napkins.
        It is out of phase. Too much exuberance.

        If which part is equal to   concentration of objects
        breath takes in parts of concrete and plastic
        lightweight aluminum frame is covered: it will be a wall
        it falls at wind/water/tide   ultralight support system
        comes up the estuaries and over the sea walls
        the first house and the next after that
        an alluvial fan of development or trailers   he sits in one and is nostalgic
        folds back knotty pine and sees the small photo
        equivocates over the environment
        as it warms, so he is warm   and cools, so he is cold
        his hand matches the cup or mug

several outdated newspapers with sections missing

sections we are missing and replaced with vacancies

sections are missing and replaced with electronic bleeps

into distance—took from there and deposited here. Over & over he writes, thinking it will lead to something. The sights of his travels are more interesting than his destination. He wavers from one site to another. The building is a choice of doors. The lightbulb is misleading. Each door faces a direction, but direction is determined by the island axis. It declares the grid within the axis. The shape declares itself into the entranceway. He walks and walks and comes to an out-of-phase street. Rather than the origin of a country

The train pulls up and is not there   if you were tree stand still for your rendition
                written in particulates   except I had been given tasks

how is the light on all the time   or you want the light to be on all the time
but the offices are dark, window after window. Glass-fronted steel skyscraper is all one-sided reflection. It could mean soft-sided but is always tempered. Shaped by what occurred afterward and there is another skyscraper pictured in that one. One half or one side of a skyscraper on the side of another skyscraper. One becomes two or one and a half, or a skyline.

The compass didn't work, so he found something in the glove compartment that acted as a directional. He didn't know the axis had been redefined. Then he took the side mirror off.

Seven clicks and hundreds of SLECOs. At first they replaced and now they are to be replaced, slowly, rather than the first big rush. Now it is haphazard, one at a time. Replaced each time with something different. Long-armed, or triplicate. Underneath it is more convenient and more congested. It was a loop like that.

One click and we'll be there. Just the underpass.

Every single part of the drawbridge had broken
Grasses bend in the silver chemical views
He said he was frozen here for hours
It grew to seem still like that

The limestone is pristine on the north-facing side and then streaks appear behind the jutting edge. Large noises from the other end of the long raw space. The windows are cross-hatched to the length of wires. Reflections reach the full length of the building—even to the *nth* floor. When will the elevator become questionable again? The space loses some of its mystery. The other side is intriguing now— across the airshaft. How you can see through windows to the other side and more windows. No impediment. He writes too close to it. Comes too near it. It was intended, by being in this site, to produce something akin to it. But it can mean anything—since—it—can. Developers prefer a level medium. No debris. This could be why it is unbuilt. Why it may never be rebuilt. By saying it, you've already designed it. It will not be random or opaque again.

Is one easily replaceable by another? Or do lights turn on while the sun is still setting? It is light against light but sky is the lightest of all.

Windows shake a little in the wind or some ground vibration. Ascent ropes move from side to side. Starting from two small red lights at top of small skyscraper, move up from pinkish-blue-white, to pale blue, to lavender cloud, to wispier clouds, to deepening, but still very bright, blue. Now becoming more scarlet, but nothing like two small red lights. Bright, but not generated. Vivid, but not emitting. Not blinking or shaking a little in the wind.

Not conducive, but a small skyscraper. A small example of it. Bright building, bright street. Dark hallway, dark alley. Some light up as others darken. And swept away. Old building, crooked street.

Found a wall a few days ago and tried to keep it away via plywood from inspectors and archaeologists. When they showed up, refused to tip the boards over and said no wall existed at all. Despite the photographs—such surreptitiousness! Note to self: Dock leaky workers.

> a few neon letters joined together
> one lamp a beacon in a window
> are you compelling me to join you on the corner
> up the elevator and through the door

It finishes so much longer than when it started. Continues over small hills and presents a dry but still glimmering aspect. Is that a mesa? Scale is impossible to tell.

One set of rivets is bare and the other plastered with grout. The drop is terrifying, momentarily. The seat is uncomfortable. Small details become large issues. Did someone adjust it while I was *not here*? I'm contemplating a wander down to the old wall. Will it be bare or will it be visible? Is it under a patchwork of boards? What we build with now. Versus cobblestone. Always rusty springy metal sticking out, and faintly discoloring material. Bent strangely. Ubiquitous concrete barriers. Always rusty springy metal sticking out. Dissolute barriers. Simple oppression with complicated and chaotic interiors.

They were lined up to keep out water.

But they are not impervious.

Who thought concrete was impervious?

The architect who built with it. Many leakages and discoloration. But beautiful structures. They treat the round shape as a club.

The gravel as convincing.

Iron as supportive, vanadium as communicative.

Bicyclists are led down open streets that suddenly turn into closed alleys. The skyline turns into something too high to scale. To be run down, herded, corralled, and led to the hooked building.

The edge of the desk is uncomfortable.

Everything is too high or too low. They hung the paintings too high.

Now we can hardly see them. Now we break up the fight.

Later, it may appear in the papers, or it may not. They leave the paper on the seat for the next person to read while waiting. Or, as they open the door, wind blows out the entire paper, every section.

Is the interior of a concrete barrier really planned? Why does it escape, bend, and oxidize? A sort of brutish reminder. Of what? Lack of foresight, of stages, of concern. It didn't keep much out, except us. We were kept out.

Once we were let out, we weren't let back in. Now we hover around the periphery. It was a wall; now it's a congested highway. On the hot asphalt, we drink bottled water. It's not a respite.

We could be unresponsive. Have every billboard blend into one. They all might advertise the same thing. What they haven't figured out is deprivation. They date them and leave them up way past the date. Through one I see a tiny lamp within a square. It must colorize the world like a movie.

The curving wall of windows prevents bookcases or a television. All that is available is the view. The light changes on the building opposite me. In one window is a reflection of an oblique circle with a diagonal trail out of it. The next time I look it's gone. The light is crawling up the skyscraper across the disaster zone. Where drivers slow down even if they don't take their eyes from the road.

As if distant it floats on the water. Another spot. Thought of as constantly rainy. A fog from another city drifts in from the ocean. Warmth at another time of year. Shining in its own reflections.

Of this there are many. It's not the only city. On every coast and inland. As if in a sink it pours in. The barges along the shores. Spirals underneath. It breathes with the seasons. When seasons stop.

She walks and comes upon a group of men
about to fight. When she comes between them
and breaks it up. SLECOs trail off into
the distance. The mysterious site: blasting zone
and conveyor belt. A truck parked partway on
curb. Even from a distance.

As if it pours in. Spirals and along a thin line. At night it sighs along the cornices. Reflects prettily in the waters. One more rivet in a plane full of rivets. And another. It's not the only one.

Light crawls from building to building. Unable to tell which is river and what is shining roof. One building is across and the other is close. Together they form a receding perspective, rather than a shimmering field of grain. A complicated composition of rectangles and odd shapes. Colors like gray, aquamarine and false red. Rather than gold-green stretching away.

Once he discounted façade maintenance. Now with background happy music the co-op votes to accommodate the nearby development. Close buildings even closer. Drilling and blue sheeting. Banging and dropping bag of CDs down stairwell. Fire escape steps fall at night or while rescuing cat. It's a chance to see dismantling close up. But the question is whether to climb while the elevator is broken or brave the acetone plume?

As it pours in she leaves. Avoid the sudden flood. You couldn't wait, could you? It had been unexpected for a while. It was what she saw while bathing in a tub filled with buckets of water she had brought down the hallway from the multi-stalled bathroom. She bathed in front of the floor-to-ceiling windows. A view of the river bend and all the highways. She bathed as though surrounded by water and city. She was immersed and surrounded by ruin. None of it had the same source and it came from the upper reservoirs. The island was criss-crossed by streams and creeks at some point. It all had the same sound.

Then the water tunnel.

Lead paint flakes into the tepid waters.

If your ability to hear bells is affected

by the noise of other people

or a beeping

by the noise of other people

continuous through floors and floors about you

as it pours in

Nature has lost its complexity   and cities now produce
an "almost" infinite number of scenarios   of chaos, contradiction, and fusion
the apparent lushness of the landscape hides "an appalling blankness"
but not here close to the clover-leaf designs, or the barriers, or the structural supports

Not counting off the top of the head, but an actual census of "ornamental" and
escaped species; in the second part of "ornamental" there *was* a heron of some kind
next to the unloading docks and oil compartments, perched on the gravel crumble
and concrete slabs left behind by the dock or old walkspace

When he told them he had cut the plants' leaves off and put them into the oven and
baked them—*all* of the office plants, the snake plant, spider plant, philodendron,
and asparagus ferns (messy)—they immediately failed the lie detector test. What
had they been lying about?

The plant study had been conducted in a corner office. It was reportedly reflected
in a window across the street. There were only two floors rented to the company
that had built the building and all the rest were rented to small businesses.

A tiny hole was burned into a leaf by one of the electrodes for the study. It affected
the results, but not more so than when the plants went into "deep faints" when
someone thought skeptical or questioning thoughts about the study.

Plants do not tolerate questioning or skepticism, apparently.

And go into a "deep faint" where they are completely unresponsive to you. The only defense is to be even more unresponsive to them. After all, they'll need water eventually. Or repotting.

every microbe has a soul

and can read your mind

Introduction: I do not believe I am a part of it. Rather, I believe I run counter to it. As then there is now a countercurrent. There is always a paradox. There is never an exception to every rule. Your opposite exists simultaneously with you. The culture wafts like an air current. It is slightly visible when electrified by your aura. We are never all part of a monolithic X. A monolith is made of very tiny parts. Small marks, disintegrations, scratches on the surface. Increasingly complicated solutions to simple problems.

Subjective and contradictory belief systems. Frictionless wheels. Vacuum. Clearance. Contamination of one medium by another. Never purely paint and never purely sculpture. The large financial systems. Paying for it. Spandrels apply as much here as anywhere. There is no reason to be discursive about this. Working on the wheel. It is the city: it shifts and resettles along new indices, then becomes itself again. Don't miss the ρ explanation of the walls. A multitude of variables all sizes. Mist and more mist until the tops of skyscrapers are lost in mist.

As this is always. Do you believe that? Once it is said it is no longer true.
As if it ever were. I seem to have that ability. You say. To state that which
is true and is now exactly not true. Don't you trust me? To have your city
then take it away. I understand your extreme dislocation. I can travel from
one city to another in under 20 minutes. The city is a continuum, but not
exactly like another. Landscapes are not a continuum. Vernal pools here,
then drought a few steps away. Wildlife huddles as though on an ice floe. If
they step off: cars, trucks, trailers, gasoline, antifreeze, hunters, government
agents, mining interests, ranchers, rat bait, cyanide runoff, trailings, bureau
of land management, jeep jamborees, hikers, construction workers, gated
communities, letters to the editor, feral cats, feral hogs, spotted knapweed,
kudzu, norway maples, starlings, industrial parks, speed limits, natural gas,
methane extraction, timber lobbyists, landfills, drunk driving. Etc. It's just
what I thought of first. I needed a few examples. Nature is a discontinuum.
Fragmentary microclimates. Islands. If the only ship stops coming and then
what happens. Axes of less quality made from smaller clam shells, seeping
springs, and a fast decline in land birds. A dry but still aspect.

Surrounded not by surf, but by itself. The city looks across its wharves and sees
not commerce but another city. Wages are shrinking there but increasing here.
The city pays better but is paying less. It lies across the surf and surrounds itself. It
comforts itself in its developing embrace. Would like to see taller towers where it
sees itself. Across the shores it binds itself. It makes itself more secure in boundary
areas. Does not bristle so much as connect. On paper, wharves make it look like a
porcupine, but that which seems spiny is actually antennae. On paper, it is upside
down and circles again north and south.

What acts as a mirror to a city? When it is a continuum how can a reflection be created? It continues itself but does not see itself, and will never see itself because it won't end. Or can reflections stop unchecked growth? If outside the city reflects the city, will the city look and stop? As the skyline across the shores reflects the skyline, will it then? To send in an imitation of itself. To confront situations it would rather not be in. A sort of reflection but more of a necessary recreation. How the city is like ourselves. The sound reminds us of rain. The rain simulacra begins. And surrounds us with reflective waters.

The skyscraper appears to breathe as light crawls over its reflective surfaces. From hundreds of windows people look out over the shores, rivers, and acres of grasses. I see it from a distance so can only guess at the buckling and distortion glare on its miles of aqua glass. And rooftop air conditioners, interior heating systems, engineered cross-shock dispensers. A faint wiggle of distortion at its very top: the venting apparati at work. A small flame burnt once . . .

and saw it from another office, this one blocked up or facing an airshaft. Like a dream in which walls were prefabricated. Wall after movable wall brought out the door and fed into a trash compacter. The fine dust covers her each day as she walks by. And later she finds her desk and books covered in ash.

Like the tedious film they watched at the opening. It looped the same images, which weren't that interesting to begin with. Outside there was at least one construction project per block. A matter of permits. Too many of them. She thought she'd chronicle each project per day. It was a project on projects. But it doubled back on itself and got nullified. That's what happens when everything in a city is documented.

It becomes opaque.

In every direction. It is written in a different space. So it is not *site-specific*.

It arrives in an oblique green space.

That was what they were looking for. In the proposal. It had to adhere to the *area*. Engage the *location*. He writes site over sight as though it would be illuminating. Corners are not good enough on their own but must be enhanced. Or aggravated. Decoration everywhere and a sound like bird calls from the ceilings. Inside the concrete warehouse were imitations of nature, including a magnetic fountain everyone found irresistible. Needles hung in a star-shape facing inward. People kept pointing, moving their fingers closer and closer, but not touching. Outside, the sunset was somewhat obscured by low storage containers that should have been dismantled. Then clouds were only glimpsed between bridge lattices because, you see, we were directly underneath them. How unspeakable to see a bridge rise from the end of a street.

Later we reduced back to human scale and entered a chocolate shop in anticipation of dinner. The sun had already set and clouds were invisible in a navy-black sky. Only the bridges continued being illuminated. Those, and the skyline on the other side. Where we were returning again. Growing large and city-like.

Je suis un éphémère et point trop mécontent citoyen d'une métropole crue moderne . . .

I jingle coins in my palm as I stroll the streets of my unending childhood. I have never become a man. I have never let go of childish things. My discontent buds and blooms on a routine basis: often several times per day. I lack the softness that is developed by the ease of mechanical things. Unlike the echoes that surround me, I am both aware of and obtuse about sudden events. The unsteadiness of a man walking toward me alarms me; the distant sounds of explosions mean nothing. We walk together in the same direction, downtown. We return home at night together, uptown. Slightly southwest and then slightly northeast. We walk arm in arm, as the sidewalks were designed to accommodate. They were designed to accommodate four people walking abreast. They were designed for you, me, and two more friends. Or I weave around three others, four, five, six who fill and overspill the sidewalks. All the thousands who fill the sidewalks.

Rien de riche.—La ville!

Groups of people look at it; cars slow down. They forget about their destinations. Thinking about them might lead somewhere—else. As we climb down from the woods, the path grows less rocky; there are fewer fallen branches and vines. Then, abruptly, the path is cultivated: we are surrounded by lawn and garden. The grass is green and the undulations of the land are gentle.

le faubourg se perd bizarrement dans la campagne

Pockets of springs, every acre a spring. From primitive springhouse to fountain. Spouting out of horse mouths or over giant frogs. In a courtyard enfolded within an alley overhung with cultivated plants in another part of the neighborhood and shuttered windows and attic quarters. A gray light pierces through skylights in which the glass is wired, making small parallelograms. Or they sandblast the façade, again. Years later, dust from the "event" still sifts in through closed windows. Later that day she returns to find her desk covered in ash.

It is not *site specific*. Every proposal has to find a way to make exploited areas meaningful again. Even surrounded by developments and land-usage plans and township restrictions, the proposal must be *site specific*.

To be *site specific*: Enhance your understanding of the area. Artistic intervention in a "specific locale." Rehabilitation of brownfields? Industrial park! Exploited, developed, "privileged sphere," extracted, gentrified, strategic. Prairie park. Desert orchard. City monument.

I am going back to work and you ask directions. Let me tell you a story about giving directions. Two people of indefinable gender stopped to ask which way the old wall uncovered by recent transit authority construction on a cross-harbor tunnel was. He couldn't remember the historical significance of the street name so he told them to look for large landmarks by which they could steer. They were so bundled up against the cold all he could see was their eyes. They wanted to know where the closest public library was and he had absolutely no idea, so he told them to continue 12 miles down until they came to the pizzeria, at which point they were to turn left and continue onto the bridge, even though dusk was falling.

More stories about giving directions: The sailboat was supposed to be a fun ride on a soft summer night, until ferries trapped it between a tanker and a barge. The couple walked so far they came to a mall. A mall, in a city! Even if they had taken books out of the library, they would never have been able to return them. He was pretty sure they had accents. And when they asked him to take a photo . . .

Well, and the old wall was covered with blue sheeting and plywood. Even now they're still looking for it.

Or ropes swinging outside the window. A bad sign, indicating scaffolding and façade sandblasting to come. They appear at night and wield blasters over the faux limestone exteriors. Then you return to find chunks of decorative elements embedded in the sidewalks in front of the door. That's the hazard of a city. In high winds, metal takes off and flies. An upward swirl of wind lifts napkins, wax paper, paper bags, and newspapers. They reach to the *nth* floor and then sail out into the harbor.

In the other space gray light filters through the skylight. No view of skyscrapers, no light falling across a façade, no faint glint of river, nothing. Just an oblique track of fluorescent light above the air conditioner. Pools of water in plastic protecting against the dust. A space when you should be in the other space. You long for it. The space you want to be. Although if you were in that space, you would want to be in the other space. It's like that, equally divided. The wind fills one part of the sail while the current pulls at the other. Each space is almost imaginable in your mind. As though to be there was to commute and discover only a shed. To commute via rail or flight, or walking 20 minutes to be in an extension of the same city, or another city. That's why the suburbs are unimaginable. The same street curves around in intentional design. Design by one person makes it unimaginable when you are not him or her.

A conglomerate of mutual designs, a hodgepodge, a chaotic street structure built one upon another, makes it imaginable, or at least one can dream about it.

Je suis un éphémère . . .

It arrives in an oblique green space.

How amazing to witness all this construction in one year. The steam cranes pump pilings into the ground, as wooden planks are inserted to hold up dirt. Not everyone who walks by eyes it for arrowheads or small beads.

All of that was already taken, as when the original bargain was made.

All this construction in one year. A ladder crashes through the glass historico and everyone exclaims. Luckily it was on the dark side of the street, so no one was walking there. The entire city often feels like a *balloon frame*: wood, flammable, if combustion begins we'll spread one to the other, we are here together and conduct construction like electricity . . .

as though we are electrical creatures

shocking each other

and linked as though through outlets

conducting relative to one another

a network, a web

of our communal electricity

as though we are outlets

or currents

and combustible in a way

electricity is not combustible in itself

we electrify ourselves

with our own electricity

no levels of wattage, no buffers

but directly one to another

current to each other

as the city catches fire

and explodes

visible to suburbs and exurbs, and settlements after those

and dark outlying areas very far out

a column of electrical fires

and bridges opening

as though we were water

as though once more living here could become ecstatic

*

Now my desk is bare and I can get on with it.

The dust has been wiped away and the ash—

The view is the same, the buildings are the same. Soon they will be documented at
each stage of reflection. Each time the light changes, they will be documented.

l'éclat impérial des bâtisses, et la neige éternelle du sol

through the seasons, through a year . . . the sun moves closer to its zenith,
and heats the skyscraper peaks. They melt, and a small wiggle distorts the clouds
behind them. Plastic slides down a measurement at a time and joins with the metal
substructures beneath it.

direct glare gives way to shadow thrown by tall building;
scent of seawater as eyes are submerged into false dusk.

if the building had been designed to carry itself as a load   and then unseemly
cannot handle or brace deserving of reflection or light over its surface   wheeling
imitation of stars   foundation square upon the "lot" and upper stories carry a tale:
of presenting itself to a harbor as a certain entity, with secrets lodged between each
enameled brick

revealed in public space: where the brass line ends and civic interaction begins
if the human is on that line and sleeps

then he is untouchable

*

at the time the project was developed there was concern about depending so
completely on a non-renewable resource and it was *strongly* suggested that an
alternative resource be used: the problem was that the alternative did not at all
perform the same function as the initial resource and would in fact be completely
impractical. Allow me to tell you the specifics: when it was planned that the
railroad should be extended through the country, critics suggested that the trains
run on *granite tracks*

rather than iron

iron being non-renewable

the country would then be dependent on another country

which was true

in the same way the city is dependent on the country

if the city is much like being another country

it made sense to be walled

and still does

to have a *walled city*

being as all of the non-renewable resources appear to flow in

and only come back in unrecognizable form

iron can be made to look like anything

including granite

you may not know it

but we ride on granite

*

It was a street that had the aspect of a gate; two buildings seemed to guard the street, which dead-ended at a park. The name of the street was also the name of the neighborhood. Residents went through phases in their feelings about the street. At first, they decided to live there after visiting because they liked it so much. Then they grew to hate the street, finding it tacky, loud, and touristy. After some time, they started liking the street again, remembering

what it was that first drew them to it. When they were lonely, or tired, or
hungry, or feeling their years, they walked down the street toward the park
and watched all of the people and looked in the store windows at the clothes,
books, and music. When they had out-of-town visitors, they took them
first to this street, but ate their meals at restaurants on other streets as, no
matter how many years passed, they could never reconcile to how bad the
restaurants on this street really were, even though they used to eat at them
when they were young.

le jour mat produit par le ciel immuablement gris

Coming across the floor to greet us
if written as close to the progression
when sun comes blinding in
could that adhere or be as precise
surely there is something *true*
if written as close to the progression
now light is changing across where I am
I have observed it on others and now it changes me
if I chronicle the progression
surely there is something *true*

but looking closer
it changes surfaces
but does not change within itself
location changes quicker than intensity
although intensity will change
not as noticeably
and later it will be quite noticeable

does not change the surface itself

although it will

right now it does not

it appears powerful

it is seen as powerful

and it will be powerful

but right now it does not change the surface

not this second

I will go stand in front of it

and surrounded

and in that way I should look upon the city and its skyscrapers

even in the direct beam of heat and light

and the skyline appears as through a haze

created on the windowglass

of its own dissolution

as the molecules are made of it

and seeing it shall be in grand scale

and intimate as dust splotches on glass

rubbed on my fingers

and haloing the view

the view of skyscraper, sky, cloud, river, and dustpit

dustpit where skyscraper was and were

had been

a constructed dustpit, constructed out of what had been where

and were

but my glass of water is over by the window
despite writing that I would stand there I didn't
and the beam moves slowly over from where I should have been
but wasn't, to things I talk about seeing when I am not seeing
it takes a moment of looking and another minute of writing
then another moment of looking and more minutes of writing
yes, a million things could happen in that minute or moment between looking
and writing
it is still linked to this *site* and is still *specific*
while I would like to believe I am not here in that split-second between absorbing
            and transferring
I am, and my water sits over by the window
absorbing that to which I am not attending
there is always time and never time
to be somewhere in time
each five minutes has an impingement
and each second another second between it
I was not enfolded
or even warmed
where is the bus to take me home?
where can I put my bag down and gaze out the window
at the passing façades?
but the dark blue is also beautiful
and the glass becomes transparent
the light is not on it
moving inside to outside, now

*

ferries move slowly across the harbor, their lights yellow upon the blue waters
water choppy and thus glittery
reflecting more intensely the sky changing

I am waiting for your call, to be released
from inside to outside. To walk northward arm in arm
on sidewalks built for us and maintained:
some original sidewalks remain, long granite extrusions
and then newer ones, unmarked by leaf, foot or hand.

Others are sanded down and labeled with orange.
People would sue their city if they trip over its grounds
while in its environs and under its protection
it would pay them back even as they have paid.
Even as they have lived here and been part of it.
They would want more and look to the sidewalks,
their underfoot, their grounds, which lead them
from street to street and to all of the avenues.

If the dust appears again. Parts of the ceiling are falling. Trails of dust indicate
the direction of walking. Where my feet have gone. As well as yours. Released
from work and walking northward arm in arm. Waiting for such time as when
the sun moves, leaving shadows over the faces of skyscrapers. The long forms and
becoming longer. Stretching over the waters and permanent shadows. A slight

oblique turn creates an uneven parallelogram. Here he rests under a pyramid. It is that across the street.

If the dust appears again. I have cleared my desk and prepared it for onslaught. From outside comes the ground-up molecules of everyday action. Aware of and obtuse about sudden events. The distant sounds of explosions mean nothing. Yet enter through the window and land on the desk. Like being pushed to do something and having an entire city watch you.

Seeing many things and some terrible too. It had the aspect of a gale, and reflected in multiple fissures as such. If it sounds like it is raining, then that affects the surrounding perception of media. It was condensation and it felt like thousands of people. It was an immediate fog and each light was given a decision.

Walking northward and even more. To see the darkness of the outlying areas. The intentional street designs. Commercial and industrial zoning. The foot of a bridge and no more. Pedestrian area and then wharves and warehouses. *The suburb melts strangely into the country* as cultivated gardens melt into scrubby, second-growth woods. Part of a deer leg edges onto a coyote corpse left by the side of the peripheral highway. Curled up by the exit and then missing when we finished visiting the city museum in the patch of old woods. We saw it and then it was pushed into the estuary reaching past three cities along the river. Tipped over the side of the peripheral highway with concrete boots on, and later to be rediscovered with miles of tangled fishing lines and smooth grass where brambles used to be.

It was like that, the flood, and three cities reach up the estuary to where salt water blends into fresh. Where the invertebrates clean the vertebrates and keep the entire body clean. The salinity controls and thermometer. As the water unfurls in front of us.

Gray against green:
light greens between dark greens
and in another season, browns, golds, oranges, reds.
A plurality of colors, contrasted
against the gray striped with yellow.
Does the road lead away from water?
Will it lead us deeper into land?
Away from the city and its hundreds of satellites.
The boroughs, the suburbs, and the feeding exurbs.

Away from the *great canals, tremendous views of modern coastal defenses,*
the *promontory*

we walk
into the continent comprised
of old rock and sediment, fossils, compacted, minerals, jewels, metal, and oil
humus, roots, threads, but
it is not as though the interior were uninhabited
there are cities below cities and below the stretching plains
and there is water: great underground aquifers
springs along coal seams

we arrive in an oblique green space

after days without traffic and days without weather
simply perfect clouds in an imminent blue sky
it was like that, the clouds

but there was a subwoofer tremble
a deep-throated rumble

slower than we had thought and
faster, too
we

   it was imaginary: it was not imagined
   an opening in a hallway down which
   you could see a lightbulb. Like a place where
   lights are left on all of the time. Constant orange
   glow. Before the ocean is the skeleton of a building-to-be.
   Upon it they build. And each floor strung with a small bulb.

   While we thought we could escape the city
   outside is only the highway and the bridge

   the moat and the moat that contains water, fish, and concrete boots
   and shopping carts and tires and boots and wood and plastic baggies.

   The same persistent, pervasive hum.
   To come to the island you cross a mile of salty water
   and climb over inhospitable embankments
   snarled with fishing line and splintering wood stumps
   and trespass a highway with not one stoplight
   or hitchike through a tunnel
   choked with carbon monoxide fumes, or worse
   rickety mineshaft—of—
   cough, cough.

it was like that, the wave
and trees clutching at air, and plastic baggies

she tries to open the window, but it is locked and bits of paint/ceiling/plaster
shower on her. If the window would open, she could throw out a rope ladder
and investigate the lower roof with its slate bowl set underneath a giant
faucet. Then next to the eagle statues that look over the narrow street and
to the harbor. The eagle shapes capture the light bounced off water on three
sides. Because it is a *promontory*. At this point it ceases to be an island.

toward it, as point comes together comprised of all that goes before it

not only the water reflects, but as sun goes down, there is a moment—
light bounces off a neighboring skyscraper—ugly in itself, black and grey
light bounces and comes back to window
creating translucent violet shadows of knapsack, books and lamp (already this time
of day) and reflects off drywall, usually matte white and at this second
gypsum crystals glitter, one vein in particular, but light passes quick and glitter
changes to slight shine, trail, now tinted rose, and a gleam on wall.

Then turn to streetlight below and skyscraper on horizon now captures light
light angles up aquamarine glass façade, sky still brightly blue

as a day passes so does the writing of it

*

The city is made of untouchable facets.

When drenched it becomes unbearably active.

Each facet reflects another part of itself

but never self-reflective: always moving *out*.

More rain, until every surface reflects

The dry floor inside—oblique concrete slabs patterned with absent tiles. Their long lines contradict their short shadows. Above the shadows of absent floorings rise concrete islands. He sits in his space and plots how to link islands to one another. Is that just a description of where he is?

Can we enter the other space and then come back to this one?

I look across the airshaft and debate electrical currents. Some people removed the plastic guards from their bulbs. Not perpendicular, but not parallel either. We have been given the task of renovating this space. But we are reminded it's not ours. In the morning, our papers are scattered on the floor. Handprints on our desk. Stirring up the dust and shadows. The role of the landlord is. To prevent building.

While the windowsill remains clean, there is dust and small bits of plaster on the desk. My elbows are white with it. I look over to the wall. It is the street. It is a wall. People go to it and walk in place.

The view includes protesters. They don't want anything to be built in that space. It is *their* space. The problem is that it is also *our* space. Is it just a description of where we are? We respect them, but they don't respect us. I used to respect them. Now I just watch. It is just a view. A sight. Drivers slow down as they pass. Their destination is more important to them than their travels. But they still slow down as they pass.

We mill around. It is very loosely organized. Each day, debris accumulates. Out of skyscrapers come piles of mud. Doorways are filled with it and men in masks cart it into dumpsters. Then where do the dumpsters go? Over the bridges or under the harbor. They block the tunnels with dumpsters. It is a wall and we go at it. We meet it with our bodies. They go to it and pass through. Parts of the wall allow it. It depends on the light.

If it surrounds us, rather than water. To find harmonics in it.

Once this neighborhood was many neighborhoods. On old maps there are indications of early bridges. But nowhere else. And now we say we have built the very first bridge. *We* are the bridge-builders. When I walk through this neighborhood, I walk through many unnamed neighborhoods. The stone neighborhood. The arched neighborhood. The furred neighborhood. Now I am in the walled neighborhood. All around us is—

It could only be improvements. Capital improvement programs. Phrases we never use and which pop out from nowhere. Capital gains improvement programs. But we still don't get them quite right. Like we don't inhabit them fully. Capital improvement systems. Gains. Capital. Systems. Improvements.

The process of rebuilding. Men pour pitch into a beat-up bucket and point flamethrowers at it. Mud is carted out from every doorway and poured into dumpsters. The pitch-flamethrower scene is from the past. We will remember it and think of the days of pitch, grease, oil, open flames, exploration, construction.

An open flame on a warmish early spring day. Just as wood planks part the soil and expose piping. It was like that the day before it happened. Before drivers slowed on the way to their destinations. After we saw the lightbulbs and scaffolding go down. As you walk through it and leave trails of where you have been. The damage is visible and expanding. Your feet are part of it. They carry for miles what you have been through.

There was not so much gray stone, but a wall with traces of a house on it. A "ghost" in this city absent of ghosts.

as point comes together comprised of all that goes before it

The saw starts up and ends. Silence. The saw starts up and ends. Then chipping. Grinding. A hammer.

Jackhammer.

Printing presses—clunk, clunk!

Jackhammer again.

Staple gun. Duct tape unscrolled. Rip!

Footsteps moving overhead. The sounds of dragging. And crash! Something fell on
the floor.

What could a neighbor possibly be doing?

More neighbors. Neighbors all around. Cities that accommodate thousands.
Sidewalks, ceilings, stairwells that accommodate thousands, millions.

j'ai cru pouvoir juger la profondeur de la ville!

To dilute sun with a lamp. The incandescent bulb is warm and 60 watts. Behind
it the wall is blue with sunlight. Even bluer than it once was. Across, the wall
speckled with sun. Curved, in reflection, off the small curves of windows. Of the
windows where I am.

Two parallels. Facing the harbor. Everywhere an angle. Something reflected in our
faces. If alone then surrounded by low buildings. Like an eight-lane bridge. If alone
then surrounded by low buildings "like a city of pigeons" gray and at constant war

with alleys. One brings others. If alone then never surrounded. But towering over. If a pink and blue city, then waves. If historic downtown protected, then X feet. Then too low and will never happen again (she says with total conviction). Then more of them where it happened and much higher with more windows.

Then more of them where it happened and much higher with more windows.

Because that's the way it is on the promontory.

Knowing what is going to happen. And preparing for it. Pigeons head out in flocks.

But we stay.

Having prepared for it.

She returns to her desk to find it covered with dust. But unevenly, with plaster bits clustered around her books. The center is clean, while postcards are fuzzed by fine dust. Before anything can take place, it must be cleaned. Through a bevy of small actions. And straightening up.

Outside, "the view." She performs ablutions and little exercises in front of the evacuation crater. Protesters stand next to the chain-link fence. In the foreground is a park being built. Benches and trees are already in, while the ground is still planked.

Protesters stand next to the chain-link fence. Whether they are inside or outside. Concrete barriers with rusty springy metal sticking out. But I am not on their side.

I am looking at "the view." A new building is compared to a symphony. It is the only new thing in the skyline. Is the skyline deteriorating? Should the eight-lane bridge empty into historic downtown? We kept missing the street in. Is that an old building? Underneath the aluminum siding. There they are, the wood shingles. This is where the inn was. And what sort of shingles are those? Asphalt, sparkling and very rough to the touch. He lived near here. And still does. Now he is hooked on something. Now we don't know what to do. We only open our door when the bell rings.

It's like that, friends.

What was that, you tried to say?

Did you try to say this:

>   all I see from the airplane is
>   squares the entire *space* has been subdivided
>   building eight-lane bridges after storms and fire devastated—
>   —devastated—   and then saying it will not happen again after
>   it just happened

Did you try

Our connection is bad. We'll try again later. In the meantime, something drawn at random: *The swaying motion on the bank of the river falls*

The book falls to the floor and is immediately dusty. The dust she swept off the desk onto the floor. The floor absorbs more dust because it is dust. The tiles have been pulled off, leaving only their patterns behind. Try to imagine that—patterns when the original is gone. Much like farms look in the winter. When they are lying fallow. And the soil created over thousands of years "regenerates."

At this point, it could become static. A seascape. Perhaps pointillist. Small colors build up to a view. The waves almost seem to lap, the sails almost billow. And close to the crater, they do. They may lap. And they may carry away candy wrappers and bits of hamburger buns. At the small beach close to the airport, people carrying a giant netted bag filled with clams assure us the tide was clean here, coming in straight from the ocean. We saw black smoke on the horizon and heard sirens. The bus driver announced he was skipping all stops. We had misjudged the magnitude of it, initially, and after all, if we couldn't taste it, it was hard to imagine it was there. The bridge to this island is often unplowed. The springs and magnetism have a certain effect on cell phones, internet access, and regular phone service. No one explains it, least of all the line workers. The same cable has been down for years at the top of the hill. After the last ice storm, the transformers were fried. Completely destroyed. A black-and-white scene. No color to it at all. Only snow and wires, and giant steel structures crumpled into fascinating patterns.

Which he studied intently. And later depicted. Or rendered. Or translated. Into his own forms. He takes the various lines and redraws them. Not in steel, but charcoal, or pencil. Steel is transformed into powdery aluminum and tree pulp. But is not only that. Metal always becomes more than it is, especially when no longer itself in form.

What could be more amazing, metal or plastic? Metal takes on plastic form, or plastic imitates metal. Glass is another plastic substance, but doesn't *give*. Instead, it slowly spills downward. Does the same go for plastic? So many kinds. Some soft and bendable, even fragile, transparent, gossamer, nearly invisible. Plastic softeners enter you and liquify you. Your deep cells and chromosomes. Wherever plastic can enter. Every letter of you. And then the other plastic, hard and edged, serrated, stronger than steel, which can tire. Plastic never tires. It harbors everything. Constructing skyscrapers out of plastic where it shimmers into metal and glass, and one is forced to wonder, which is the most reflective? *Is plastic more reflective than glass?*

The light is starting to get lighter longer
and with that longer light

things clearer that had been distant
as though on the horizon or in another domain

another locale, another region, a different quarter
keeping all the same name, similar aspect.

Another building rehabbed,
another street resurfaced.

Grinding sheetrock, masked
workers carry ceramic tiles, or I-beams.

A renovation or a gutting.
A demolition.

Each time I think you are
finished, you begin again.

What could be more physical than that? Fill up the space, they said. Make it yours.
But I am just a renter. With no "footprint" anywhere. It was sunny, with gorgeous
light, and the second time looking out the window, it had turned gray as mice.

A paper bag crushed on the sidewalk, folds and wet footprints on it. The logo is
indiscernable. Does decoding a language include decoding language in a new
form? Once again a sense of the desk slipping to one side. Books slide off one after
the other, into the dust.

As though I were just a renter. With no "footprint." Is it because the pieces of paper
are slanted? Slowly advancing to the window. An unsettling sense of—

Locale, region, quarter, domain. Or neighborhood. The good lunch places resemble
the bad lunch places.

Which only reveal themselves after a bout of stomach flu. The desk is sagging in
the middle. Or you are a perfectionist who can't spell anything. It's disturbing. It *is*
disturbing.

et de se croiser des boulevards de cristal habités incontinent

A ghost in this city of no ghosts. She put the cup back inside the other cup, and the insulating sleeve over that. It says "uses approximately 45% less material than a second paper cup" but is "intended for single use only." It came in two cups. Habits are hard to break. At the local supermarket, red-faced men bag groceries for pennies. One cannot request "paper." One cannot say "I have my own bag." And then she spilled tea over the stack of magazines and offered to pay but they wouldn't let her; later she discovered she had left the newspaper she had bought and the reason she had bent over with the tea—to fold the newspaper into a convenient half shape to carry onto the elevator.

Once on the elevator she notices a button for "PH" that had not been there in the previous version of the elevator: the one they ripped out of the shaft only went to "6." She could only go to "6" while using the stairwell for several months while the elevator was being fixed. But if she pressed it, the elevator might halt and dangle in the *hoistaway*. Even though an elevator is really a *hoistaway*. See *elevator*.

They knew her. While she thought she was unrecognizable. Just because you hide behind dark sunglasses doesn't mean the world is dark. She broke up a fight between a group of men, and then spilled tea on a pile of magazines: Baby Fights! the headlines said. In this city of no ghosts, but a lot of crazies.

Holes carved into the tops. Of very thin planks. Almost outer rings or bark. Splinters noticeable even from this floor. And locked out and entering the adjacent space. From there one can see the side lot ribbon. Halting and thoughtful at the end of each alley. As though each block had to be walked before they accumulated enough to become a city.

*

Later, because the light is quiet now, and slightly green—
we needed to see changes in the light,
measuring them with the body.
A gentle curve takes over
measured by bodies and thousands of them,
the scale of the body immeasurable
crowding the sidewalks and on line for the train
arrival is everywhere and multiple
but the light is quiet now, and slightly green
foreshadowing water and vacant spaces.
The light is changing and so are the trees.
We join the crowds on the sidewalks
more of them to see the view,
to pass by the site slowing down,
to avoid anything that might be construed as an invitation *to*

> *to* green spaces oblique and suburb
> even as the city sinks
> even as elements enter
> and it begins to drown

la soirée frissonnante trouvent notre brick en large

We cast off from industrial landscapes, the city recedes—
but here it is: tides define it. Islands disappear under
wind, and reappear under bridge, brackish and bristling.
It is undefinable, but it surrounds. The city would be—

sprawl without ocean. It is delineation and necessary.
In return it scatters to it. Glass goes out and comes in.
Over the curve, the first apex appears.

Light glitters on the waters
and an orange glow on the horizon before that.
Blinking light, metronomic. And another.
Once you return: can it be achieved—in various space?
The spire appears on the bowl horizon
now buildings now roofs
in the other space to slightly different sounds
as if it were something to be *carried with you.*

*

Like that you could leave it.
The spire appearing on the bowl horizon
the sunset flattened out and reddened
stars small spikes in an orangish sky.
If you were going to prepare for it
refer to it, then you knew it could be—

the same as farther out, as in other spaces
each time you thought it was final, an end
another development, construction, a new skyline.

You never expected it to be altered
that it would be filled with hammering sounds
and sawdust and people coming back.

But *I* am just a renter.
Gazing at crossbeams segmenting the small views.
The length of the street opening.

This is my space and so am I. Because I divide
doesn't mean it can't be constructed anywhere. Because
I have a view. And that view was reproduced and is still.

*

It does not reveal upon viewing
gaze and gaze upon it, or look quickly and then away
the mechanics of light when splintered by construction
plastic is not crystalline, nor is metal *intentional*
some of it is planned, and mixed with the not-planned
a master-plan of substructures, detailing each lock-box, tube, dutch wall
or many plans, some forged and aged with vinegar and charring at the edges
fingerprints, bullet holes, and sawed bits
which plan is which and development must proceed
drill here and find a nest of rats with tails entwined
our mirror peoples, one per person, or one per acre, or at least one per block
all of which need to be walked, and charted, and documented here
do we imbue more than necessary? very well, then we imbue
as cities are meant to be imbued and take on the patina of hordes—

un bras de mer, sans bateaux . . .

Yesterday's paint dried nicely, but now I only see missed spots to be repainted.
Along the bottom of the walls runs a splotch of blue paint; on the east side, a

splotch of red. The black radiator shows through the sloppy paintstrokes of the previous tenant. Along the edges, the rollers' gap is evident. Spackle soaks up paint and remains grayish yellow. The sponge brush doesn't fit in the small can and rips on a hidden nail. Outside the window, the same. An open pit with yellow dirt. Paint cans and bags of plaster, beginning to tear and exhaling dust. Small leafless trees with plywood about them, outlining where the root systems must be. A few tentative benches. Of a different design. The new one is still on the table. They discuss and come to another conclusion. Later the plans will be redrawn. It took some warming to come to that.

Now the paint can is closed and sealed.

With its own paint. Its latexity. Inexplicably washable in water.

But when it rains.

Wanting to have the blue splotch in the upper righthand corner explained, but unable. She turned to books, one of which was recommended. The grayness faces a plethora of violets and reds. It is an obstacle to sunset, and therefore to viewing. It prevents the change of day, and thus, an ending.

Sounds grow louder and overwhelm.

As gray becomes blue and lighter still. As light comes closer and edges out things. Things being built or designed. Edging out or lining. As blue becomes green and then yellow. At the top of perceivable bowl, a demi-circle or one part of what surrounds us. Looking high and what is above buildings and skyline. What is lined by sky. Yellow and then metallic. Compared to metals so is light as close to what we think *gleams*. To imitate a gleam.

As it comes closer. Like that I or you am part of a wall. If a wall, lost, is the easiest thing to track. If the wall were lost. Then what *lost* means. When regarding structures. Unbuilt, taking papers down until revealing minute holes left by tacks? A larger rupture caused by nail hammered on other side? Some display feathered expansion, while others are self-contained void, but all evince pattern constellation. Figured by trace of drawing hung.

To imitate a gleam. When building with transparent materials? Patterns from old projects? Or debris?

Is that what lost *when regarding structures* means? What *lost*? Which *loss*?

Minute holes left by tacks. Then repainting. Toothpaste applied with a toothpick to each tiny hole, to refill. To re-enact the wall. Then repainting but previous tenant still shows through. Still red, blue, and yellow comes through white as white dries. Why primary colors? What project before my project?

Was it a spectrum? Some spots are tiny gray. Or long spongy lines. In joints or along corners. Two walls meet with strings of dry paint as though a kind of—

unsticking.

If it comes to two small words, or a phrase. Printed out tiny.

The reflection doubles back in a new way. Some new glittery element dislodged it. Now it cuts along wall, jumps across radiator, and along dangling wire slung across fire alarm station.

As windows slowly replace wall, a giant moon-lamp rises behind glass. One by one, skyscrapers turn on, from skyline to *constellation*.

Complex of vivid shadows. The danger is in lifting the bridges and closing the tunnels. A moat turns city into *defensive structure*. Bristling with static rather than antennae.

but with.

rather than.

close.

Complex of vivid shadows. The pale sun sets behind the skyline as I move from interior to exterior and the air becomes vivid, rather than pumped. The pale sun sets on skyscrapers, cables crossing their façades. A cable hangs. On its end a traffic light, shifting.

light fades and splits into a spectrum
hangs a darker yellow line, not a reflection and not incomprehensible
bluer away from the window, as it turns blue away from lightsource
darker than that, and translucence through intercedence of paper before wall

If it grew dusty, where did it emerge? Today the view is clear and we see green in the wreckage. Like a beacon, green amid brown and grey dust. Not a made-up color, but one you see today. Even though, and perhaps because of, cloudiness, the green "pops" and invites us into the wreckage.

So color leads us in. It functions as a kind of doorway. All winter the weather was gray. But the next day was lined with green. Even in the makeshift park, spindly trees in a sort of neatly planted line leaf. Seemingly overnight, and after a lot of rain. In a sort of neatly planted line, but one that ends at the chain-link fence. Blue skies would interrupt the clarity of the view through the doorway into the room or place. It is painted, but confusingly. At that dismantled place, one did not expect to see things painted, but instead lined with plastic or metal. One thing is preserved, but not the only thing. It may not be preserved, ultimately. But replaced with plastic or metal. From here it looks like casein paint or the color of old farmhouse rooms. But that doesn't make any sense in this place, in the basement of a center of a city. It is green and excavated. It was preserved, by chance or on purpose, but may not be there ultimately, and may be replaced with a doorway.

Everything going on around it. The concrete ramp wasn't there yesterday. And the landscaping. The spindly trees in straight lines.

For the first time, inserting something.

It trailed off and left traces of where it had been, not neatly. Messy, with hairs. Catching at things. Scattering. Piles of leaf pods in the gutters and drains. They flutter as though a snowstorm. Not neatly and clogging. The city finds the perfect tree: i.e., one that doesn't shed bark or seeds or leaves, or fruits that squash and have an odd scent. One that doesn't pile up in the drains and gutters, or skid, or people slip on it. Accommodating, the city.

> from skyline to constellation. Globe turns and takes city with it. While we
> would like to think it is endless   across the river more development until
> a *river canyon* is created   but translucent with openings and reflective
> surfaces   not like a village built into a crevice   a true *canyon*   with the river
> sawing down and maybe flooding at some point   appears to float on its
> surfaces   across, above, and below,   and around itself, as it turns.

The good intention of going down to the wharves and finding the shop someone had mentioned in passing. Then hours passing too and always still cold, even as— missing the closing time, the door was already locked. If people lock their doors, other people unlock them. While it may be your property, it is everyone's property and you deserve to have your possessions sold on the street, or someone knocking into you and pretending you broke their sunglasses and have to buy them a new pair. It's only fair. You owe them for living here. How did he know about the book, anyhow? He mentioned it and it was something you never thought he'd have read.

He said he didn't believe in ghosts even though that was what his work was about. If it's verifiable evidence then it might be found—but that's too awful to think about. Should stay just a view.

In the park is a smaller park with a marble memorial, or limestone. Most of the bas-relief has worn off, even though it is only 176 years old. Every park is quartered, or slivered, in some way. But not walled. And very private.

Scents of the city: roasted peanuts, chestnuts, grilled chicken kebabs. At certain times of the year. Wood smoke, smoke. Burning plastic. Deep timbre of urine when passing an alley.

Briefly enclosed with someone else. Scenting their traces as they exit a place. A heavy trail of perfume. Blocking the scent of concrete. Concrete when it changes, weather.

Scents of a city: Concrete when it changes, weather. Memory of concrete as rock and dust. When rained upon, releases scent of—but crushed and dusty. As dust is calmed and brought back to earth. As its scent is made more pungent. As clouds move over the site, and bring dust back to ground. Into a slurry, and puddles. As sun emerges again, hardens back into itself. Dust to slurry to concrete. A crust over an occurrence. When it all flies up and catches the light. But as sky changes again.

Shadows of clouds move over the area—but plumes of construction or actual weather?

Against the wall, shadows move. Actual clouds are invisible, and disappear with the sun behind them. When they group together so, and they lose each other.
In place of dust, some order. Today, ramps, trucks, grass, fences, workers, rivets, rain gear.

Greenery visible taking root on sides of what is being bulldozed—or excavated. While construction was stopped, excavation or bulldozing continues.

Although it is certain vegetation will be removed later.

Replaced with more ordered plants and flowers: shrubs, bushes, small trees— perhaps flowering Bradford pears? This is only a guess. But plantains, chickweed, crabgrass multiply. Spread seeds and have endless root systems. Ugly and tough. Dissipate in a puff and scatter when touched. Even when ground underneath a boot, hunch to the soil, almost blending with it. To spring up after a good rain.

But—they *were* the first to come back. They stabilize the soil, even inches away from bulldozers.

Plumes of water vapor, or dust. Clouds mix with emissions, and paper and plastic bags rise so high as to reach the *nth* floor and then float out over the harbor. Trails and eddies, mixing, into water, into air. Cables swing and bump into the building, then bounce back over the heads of spectators, protesters, workers. Who can tell what from whom? The protester may be spectating, and then return to work later. The spectator may be protesting and return home to work later, or to the office. Always returning to work later, after spectating and protesting. And over all that, a dust devil, a small tornado of litter, a dust plume.

When it changes weather. Making a skyscraper perhaps more spectacular than it was initially. Could be dull tinted green and then transparent and watery. Does aquamarine of windows outweigh dull pink granite? Whether the skyscraper transcends itself. With the help of the weather. Don't realize how much it *sees*. Or how it will be *seen*.

While it is still in front of you. In a minute working here. What is remembered now, and later. To live inside as it is constructed. To look and then write: a moment of looking, inches away from viewing, and then a moment of writing—as if writing were recalling, but also looking.

As seen over here. As seen by you or me. By many others. Walking or driving by. On sidewalks and in streets, making left turns, and right turns, or going straight ahead onto one of the bridges or into one of the tunnels. Cresting above the city while lit on either side. If they flicker. If interrupted.

Affected by someplace elsewhere and so distant as to be almost incomprehensible. If trying to imagine someplace else. Hard to be elsewhere when one is here, *viewing*. Even in darkness or when the light changes making windows opaque when they were transparent. Once behind the sky visible and now only the glass. When one could view the sky behind the window and now only glass. When even the sky was altered behind it. When light is passing through and altered, but not actually. When it is actual. Unaffected by what you thought affected it.

After being distracted by to-do work and returning to it, suddenly. When raising one's head, whether in an office or at a table, stretching or taking a break, or not taking a break, and raising one's head and seeing light unaltered and electricity falter. When in a minute ecstatic. When in a minute living here.

Notes

The excerpts in French in italics are from Arthur Rimbaud's *Illuminations*, specifically, "Ville," "Villes I," "Villes II," "Métropolitain," "Promontoire," and "Départ." English translations are from Wallace Fowlie's 1966 edition of *Rimbaud: Complete Works, Selected Letters*, The University of Chicago Press.

More information on SLECOs or "Deskeys" (pg. 8) can be found at www.forgotten-ny.com/LAMPS/deskeylamps/deskey.html.

The "story" on pages 19 to 20 is drawn from *The Secret Life of Plants* by Peter Tomkins and Christopher Bird, Harper Paperbacks, 1989.

Whose blue glittered with a frosted silver
Like palace walls in Grimm papered with needles,*
The sands all shining in its larger concrete,
A dome compact of all but visible stars.

       — "Description of a View," William Empson

*The exact tale remains unidentified.